MOSES TH CHOSEN BY GOD

BOOK 2 (TOLD FROM EXODUS 2-4)

CARINE MACKENZIE
Illustrated by
Graham Kennedy

© Copyright Carine Mackenzie 2008
Published by Christian Focus Publications,
Geanies House, Fearn, Tain, Ross-shire, IV20 1TW, Scotland, U.K.
www.christianfocus.com
Printed in China

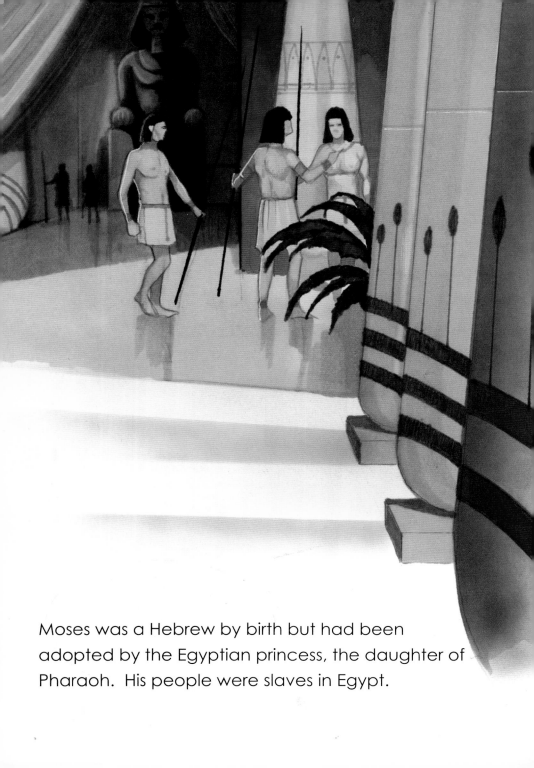

Moses was a Hebrew by birth but had been adopted by the Egyptian princess, the daughter of Pharaoh. His people were slaves in Egypt.

This made Moses angry
– he even killed an Egyptian
who was beating up one of the
Hebrew men. When Pharaoh found
out he wanted to kill Moses. Moses had
to run away.

Moses fled to the far-off land called Midian.
One day he was sitting by a well. Seven
sisters came to the well to draw water
for their father Jethro's sheep.

Some rough shepherds came and drove them away. But Moses came to their rescue and helped them to get all the water they needed.

At home, Jethro asked the girls, "How are you home so early today?"

"An Egyptian man rescued us from the shepherds. He even drew the water and gave it to the flock."

"Where is this man? Why have you left him?" Jethro asked. "Invite him for some food."

Moses then came to live in Jethro's house.

Jethro's daughter Zipporah became Moses' wife.
Moses worked as a shepherd for many years, looking
after his father-in-law's sheep.

However, God had more important work for Moses
to do. God's people, the Hebrews, cried out for help in
their slavery. God heard their prayers. He had a plan
to save them. Moses was chosen by God to be part of
this plan.

One day Moses was with the
sheep out in the desert near
Mount Sinai. A strange sight
caught Moses' attention.
He went over to
investigate.

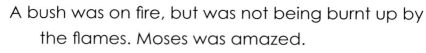

A bush was on fire, but was not being burnt up by the flames. Moses was amazed.

God's voice called out Moses' name.

"Here I am," he said.

"Don't come any
nearer," God said.
"Take off your sandals, for
the place you are standing is holy ground."

"I am the God of your fathers, of Abraham, Isaac and Jacob."

Moses hid his face – he was afraid to look at God.

God told Moses that he knew how unhappy his people were in Egypt.

"I have heard their cry. I know how they suffer. I am going to rescue them from the Egyptians. I will bring them to the lovely land of Canaan."

"I want you to speak to Pharaoh and to lead my people out of Egypt."

Moses was surprised to be chosen for such an important task.

"What if the people do not believe that the Lord God has appeared to me?"

"Throw your staff to the ground," God said to him. He did so and it became a serpent.

"Catch it by the tail," God commanded. It became a staff again.

"This miracle and others will help them to believe that God has appeared to you."

"Oh, my Lord, I am not a good speaker," Moses objected.

"I will be with you and teach you what to say," God assured him.

"Please send someone else," pleaded Moses. This made God angry.

"Your brother Aaron will work with you," God said. "He can speak well. You will tell him what to say. I will teach both of you what to do."

"Remember to take your staff, with which you shall work the miracles."

Moses agreed to do what God asked.

It is important for us also to obey what God says in his word.

Moses went to Jethro to ask permission to go to Egypt.
"Go in peace," he said.

Moses, Zipporah and their sons rode to Egypt on donkeys.

Moses took the staff of God in his hand.

God chose Moses for a special task. Moses knew he was unable to do this on his own. God told him he would be with him to help him all the time.

God chooses people still to do his will. He commands us all to repent of our sins, to turn away from them to him. We are to trust the Lord Jesus Christ for everything.